WISDOM
AND THE WELL-ROUNDED LIFE

What Is a University?

WISDOM

AND THE WELL-ROUNDED LIFE

What Is a University?

PETER MILWARD

FULCRUM
GOLDEN, COLORADO

First US publication 2009
Originally published in 2006 by Shepheard-Walwyn Ltd., London, England

Library of Congress Cataloging-in-Publication Data

Milward, Peter.
  Wisdom and the well-rounded life : what is a university? / Peter Milward.
    p. cm.
  Originally published: London, England : Shepheard-Walwyn Ltd., 2006.
  ISBN 978-1-55591-651-0 (pbk.)
  1. Education, Higher--Philosophy. I. Title.
  LB2322.2.M5 2009
  378.001--dc22

                                    2008048705

Printed in Canada by Friesens Corp.
0 9 8 7 6 5 4 3 2 1

Cover and interior design by Ann W. Douden
Fulcrum Publishing
4690 Table Mountain Drive, Suite 100
Golden, Colorado 80403
800-992-2908 • 303-277-1623
www.fulcrumbooks.com

CONTENTS

FOREWORD

Education should consist of a series of enchantments, each raising the individual to a higher level of awareness, understanding, and kinship with all living things.

—Author Unknown

*Intelligence plus character—
that is the goal of true education.*

—Martin Luther King Jr.

It is the supreme art of the teacher to awaken joy
in creative expression and knowledge.

—Albert Einstein

What is the essence of life?
To serve others and to do good.

—Aristotle

This book—a meditation on the state of our souls and of our education—was written by a man whom I am proud to call my mentor, friend, and teacher. I first met Father Milward in the early 1990s in Tokyo, when I visited the Renaissance Centre at Sophia University. Since then, I have been much inspired by his work and writings, too little known in the West.

As you will discover when you begin to read this book, he is a truly remarkable man. His charming innocence, universal compassion, and thirst for true knowledge mark him as a teacher in the great tradition of religious and philosophical sages who embrace the one universal truth. He is a giant among men who truly deserves to be described as a Renaissance man, a friend to mankind, and a bridge of reconciliation between cultures. It goes without saying that I was delighted and honored when he asked me to write the foreword.

The world of knowledge and competence is in a constant state of flux. The same can be said for the universe of visions, aspirations, and dreams. Changes are occurring every day on a national and international scale—we are faced with economic globalization, revolutions in information technology and biotechnology, growing inequality and social exclusion (leading to a renewed struggle for citizens' rights), violence of all kinds, environmental pollution, and climate change. All these things are increasing the need for new knowledge and skills, for new scenarios for our global society. Love, courage, honesty, justice, spirituality, religion, altruism, vocation, creativity—the components of life itself—are again becoming major issues.

In today's largely decadent, money-driven world, the

teaching of virtue and building of character are no longer part of the curriculum at our universities. The pursuit of virtue has been replaced by moral neutrality—the idea that anything goes. For centuries it had been considered that universities were responsible for the moral and social development of students and for bringing together diverse groups for the common good.

In the last few decades, however, and especially since the 1970s, a new generation of educational reformers has been intent on using places of learning, and universities in particular, to solve national and international economic problems. The economic justification for education—equipping students with marketable skills to help countries compete in a global, information-based workplace—has overwhelmed other historically important purposes of education.

The language of business management is now being applied to educational establishments: schools and universities are "downsized" and "restructured," and their staffing is "outsourced." But if there is a shared national purpose for education, should it be oriented only toward enhancing this narrow vision of a country's economic success? Is everything public for sale? Should education be answerable only to the bottom line? Are the interests of individuals and selective groups overwhelming the common good that the education system is meant to support?

I have been part of these changes and have witnessed their negative consequences for students and staff. An educational system that has turned students into customers or clients, pitted members of staff against each other, removed collegiality, and turned classrooms into mass-production factories, financed by profits from the sale of alcohol, cigarettes, medical drugs, and arms, has brought a bitter harvest and needs to be changed. Education has to be reunited with its roots in theology, philosophy, and the virtues.

This treatment of students as customers and courses as goods and services disregards the truly important human values and creates unhappy, purposeless, and dysfunctional people who don't know who they are or where they are going.

From 1980 onward, for the next twenty years, I taught

economics in universities, enthusiastically demonstrating how economic theories provided answers to problems of all sorts. I got quite carried away by the beauty, the sophisticated elegance, of complicated mathematical models and theories. But gradually I started to have an empty feeling. I began to suspect that neoliberal economics was an emperor with no clothes. What good were elegant theories that were unable to explain all the poverty, exclusion, racism, corruption, injustice, and unhappiness that exist in the world?

I came to feel that my life as a lecturer was like a make-believe movie: sit and relax…In the end, models dreamt up by detached economists will sort out the world's ills. My classrooms were becoming unreal places. I began to ask fundamental questions of myself. Why did I never talk to my students about compassion, dignity, comradeship, solidarity, happiness, spirituality—about the meaning of life? We never debated the biggest questions: Who am I? Where have I come from? Where am I going?

I told them to create wealth, but I did not tell them for what reason. I told them about scarcity and competition, but not about abundance and cooperation. I told them about free trade, but not about fair trade; about GNP—gross national product—but not about GNH—gross national happiness. I told them about profit maximization and cost minimization, about the highest returns to the shareholders, but not about social consciousness, accountability to the community, sustainability, and respect for creation and the creator. I did not tell them that, without humanity, economics is a house of cards built on shifting sands. Where was the economic theory that reflected my students' real lives? How could I carry on believing in such an unreal world? I could not go on asking them to believe unbelievable theories in the name of economics.

Father Milward, in the chapter "What Is Religion?," poses the question, what has religion got to do with education? A great deal...if not everything, he answers. I am delighted that he has highlighted this important but now-rejected relationship. I leave you to read his wise words on this subject for yourself to return to my own experience.

It was at that difficult time that I came to understand

that I needed to bring spirituality, compassion, ethics, and morality back into economics itself, to make this dismal science once again relevant to and concerned with the common good. It was then that I made the following discoveries, among others.

Economics, from the time of Plato right through to Adam Smith and John Stuart Mill, was as deeply concerned with issues of social justice, ethics, and morality as it was with economic analysis. Most economics students today learn that Smith was the father of modern economics, but not that he was also a moral philosopher. In 1759, sixteen years before his famous *The Wealth of Nations*, he published *The Theory of Moral Sentiments*, which explored the self-interested nature of man and his ability nevertheless to make moral decisions based on factors other than selfishness. In *The Wealth of Nations*, Smith laid the early groundwork for economic analysis, but he embedded it in a broader discussion of social justice and the role of government. Today students know only of his analogy of the invisible hand and refer to him as defending free markets. They ignore his insight that the pursuit of wealth should not take precedence over social and moral obligations, and his belief that a "Divine Being" gives us "the greatest quantity of happiness." They are taught that the free market as a "way of life" appealed to Smith, but not that he distrusted the morality of the market as a morality for society at large. He neither envisioned nor prescribed a capitalist society, but rather a "capitalist economy within society, a society held together by communities of non-capitalist and non-market morality." That morality for Smith included neighborly love, an obligation to practice justice, a norm of financial support for the government "in proportion to [one's] revenue," and a tendency in human nature to derive pleasure from the good fortune and happiness of other people.

It is heartbreaking to realize that most students' own stated wish is to be engaged more fully with religion and spirituality, but that this is ignored by university faculties. In a recent UCLA study, researchers questioned 3,680 junior students from forty-six colleges and universities across the United States about their religious commitment. While noting a high level of interest in spiritual matters among college students, the report concluded:

> There is a sharp divide between students' interests and what happens in the classroom. More than half of the students say their professors never provide opportunities to discuss the meaning and purpose of life. Similarly, nearly two-thirds say professors never encourage discussions of spiritual or religious matters…Nearly half (45 percent) report dissatisfaction with how their college experience has provided opportunities for religious/spiritual reflection.

Education is too important a field to be left to the adversarial politics of competing model builders: all such models are limited and conditioned human constructions. A correct education system must be based on a metaphysics derived from a comprehensive and unifying vision rooted in theology, philosophy, ethics, and spirituality.

There is an underlying unity between all branches of education and all aspects of learning, and this unity needs to be reflected in an integrated, holistic, and multidisciplinary curriculum that does not draw artificial lines between different disciplines. Much of modern education is still based on a machine-age model of separate subject areas, which encourages a fragmented view of learning. In the absence of a unifying spiritual perspective, inevitably little more than lip service is paid to the need for cross-curricular links.

For all those searching for new perspectives on what education should and could be, Father Milward's book is a breath of fresh air and essential reading that I can strongly recommend. He understands that, in days of spiritual hunger, education needs to do more than grope in the dark. It needs to point students to the light of the world.

—Kamran Mofid
Coventry, England

INTRODUCTION

◆

The idea of university reform is very much in the air today. But before we speak about reform for universities, it is surely necessary to go back to the ideal meaning of a university. This is something we have come to take for granted in the modern world. We all think we know what a university is, or what it should be, especially those of us who went to a university in our formative years. But what, I ask, do we really know about either the reality or the ideal of a university?

This is the question with which I begin this book, and I deal with it in two ways. First comes the more general question, what is a university? Then at each stage I ask particular questions about each aspect of university education in an attempt to go back to the beginning, to the source and origin of each word that stands for this or that aspect. For it is necessary to ask question after question, like a little child taking his first lessons in language from his mother, asking "What is this?" and "What is that?" endlessly.

These are not merely adult questions of methodical doubt, in the manner of Descartes, who for this reason has come to stand at the head of modern philosophy. For myself, I don't want to doubt anything, least of all the value of university education, so long as it is really what it is said to be. I want to begin with a sense of wonder, according to the older ideal of Aristotle, who said that all philosophy springs out of just such a sense. It is a sense of wonder that opens our eyes to the world around us and elicits questions about the things we find in that world, in the spirit of a child questioning his mother. In this sense, we have to go back, like William Wordsworth and G. K. Chesterton, to the time of childhood, when all true education, truly universal education, begins.

It is a basic mistake of what we have come to think of as a university that philosophy is regarded as a department. For philosophy cannot of its nature be special or departmental. It is universal, and all departments derive their meaning from it. As the medieval thinkers rightly maintained, philosophy is not one science among many; it is the queen of all sciences.

So now let me proceed to present the contents of this book, with the questions I propose to answer, however unsatisfactorily, one by one—according to the tested method of such great thinkers as Thomas Aquinas, with whom I cannot, of course, compare myself.

ONE

What Is a University?

◆

A sked to define *university*, someone might say, "It is a group of buildings in which students are taught various subjects for several years after graduating from secondary school." This is indeed a practical definition, but it tells us nothing about the nature or purpose of a university.

Then what, we may ask, is a university for? What is the point of having such a group of buildings and sending students there for several years after secondary school when they might be more usefully employed in earning their living?

To begin with, we may consider why we use the word *university* for such a group of buildings. What does the word mean? It may simply be said that a university is a place for the study of universal knowledge. Ideally, students at a university that is worthy of its name ought to study everything there is to be known under the sun. But of course they can't all be expected to study everything; if they were, such study would be exceedingly superficial. For what one gains in breadth of knowledge one inevitably loses in depth, and vice versa. But when students are all taken together, their separate studies may be expected to add up to everything—up to a point.

There was a time in the early thirteenth century when it could be said of a man like Albert the Great, the teacher of the greater Thomas Aquinas, that he knew everything there was to be known in the world. But that time has long since passed, if it ever existed. Now we have to admit, in the words of Virgil, that "we can't do [or study] everything."

Nowadays indeed we have come to the opposite extreme, with such an abundance of subjects, which are ever being divided and subdivided, that it is difficult for one man to know everything even in his specialized field of study, such as Shakespearean drama. Of the world of science it is said that the tendency today is for the scientist to know more and more about less and less until he comes to know everything about nothing!

Nowadays very few universities can claim to offer courses on every subject, even at a general level. But at least, to deserve the name of "university," they may be expected to offer a wide variety of courses in different fields, in both science and the humanities.

In this sense, a university of economics or a university of music, though such institutions actually exist in not a few modern countries, implies a contradiction. It claims to offer at once both universal knowledge (as a university) and specialized knowledge in one field. So it should rather be called a college or an institute.

It may be further asked what is the point of a university proposing to teach everything and then allowing itself to be divided into different faculties and departments where students study only one subject? One answer to this question, given by many universities in the United States and postwar Japan, is that for the first two years students are encouraged to take a wide variety of courses under the name of general education before proceeding to specialize in one department. Then they may be said to have been exposed at least for a time to the benefits of universal knowledge, though the common effect is rather one of universal confusion.

However, at most universities in Europe and some in the United States, as in prewar Japan, students are expected to specialize from the beginning in their chosen fields. The ideal of general education, then, belongs to secondary schools; at university, one is required to specialize.

Isn't that a contradiction? Not necessarily. All the students are engaged in the study of different subjects, and in their daily interaction they may be expected to communicate something of their special knowledge to one another. This is especially the case at universities where the faculties or departments are not divided from each other in separate buildings and where the students have every opportunity to mix with one another, as when they live together in dormitories.

For example, the University of Oxford consists of

independent residential colleges that do not specialize in any one subject but include members engaged in the study of different subjects. So while the students have lectures and tutorials separately from one another, they live together and enjoy discussing matters of common interest.

After all, even when human knowledge is divided and subdivided into many departments, the boundaries can't always be clearly defined. One branch of science or the humanities is ever in need of assistance and enlightenment from others. "No man is an island," said John Donne, and no branch of science or literature is an island either, separated from the mainland of universal knowledge.

What I have said of university students applies no less to their teachers. For a university isn't only for the education of students, who have to grow in mind under the direction of their teachers. It is also for the research of scholars, who have already achieved proficiency in their field, yet whose growth in mind is never completed. There is indeed something about knowledge that is infinite. No man, however far his studies may lead him into any one subject, however limited that subject may seem to be, can ever say he knows all there is to be known about it.

Once I met a Scottish professor whose specialized research was devoted to a certain species of fish chiefly found in the North Sea. He had been engaged in this research for the past fifteen years. I casually remarked that now he must know all there is to be known about it. "No," he protested, there remained much for him to find out. Thus, all knowledge leads to a deepening sense of mystery. As Francis Bacon said in his essay "Of Studies," "*Omnia abeunt in mysterium*"—all things disappear into mystery. The ideal of university study is to combine a broad knowledge of all kinds of things with a deep understanding of one kind, as in the pattern of a cross. One without the other is defective. Both dimensions, from top to bottom and from one side to the other, are needed for the true formation of the human mind. And then, of course, there remains the further dimension of depth, from outward to inward, not to mention other unknown dimensions.

TWO

What Is Education?

◆

L ooking into a typical classroom while a class is in progress, we may see a teacher teaching from his desk, usually on a platform, while his students sit at their desks below him. They may be listening to what he is saying, or taking notes according to his direction, or asking and answering questions—or even sleeping. That, we assume, is the process we call education. It seems to proceed from the mouth of the teacher to the ears of his students—from his mind to their minds. Thus it may be called a communication from heart to heart, as in John Henry Newman's Latin motto "*Cor ad cor loquitur*"—heart speaks to heart.

Such a process, however, should be called instruction

rather than education. It may be one means of education, but it isn't the only or the most important means at university level. Originally, in its Latin origin, *education* meant the "drawing out of" something already within the one who receives it. So what is the object of this process of drawing out? What is being drawn out in the process of education?

One theory, going back to Socrates' method of question and answer, is that it is the drawing out of knowledge. Somehow the student is thought to possess the knowledge already, in a kind of hazy, undigested form; it is for the teacher, in whom the knowledge is more fully developed, to draw it out of him and to make it more explicit and fully formed.

Such an explanation may apply very well to philosophy, at least the kind of philosophy Socrates was discussing with his disciples, or rather friends. Most people have, for instance, a vague knowledge of what they mean by such words as *culture* and *nature* and *love*, but it is for an educator like Socrates—who may not have even thought of himself as a teacher—to make them fully aware of their knowledge.

Still, that explanation hardly fits all forms of education, least of all that which goes under the name of instruction. In most classes or lectures, the teacher or professor is telling his students what they don't yet know. He is informing them, or giving form to their vacant minds. In so doing he may well be enlightening them, throwing new light on what they already know in part, but he is also giving them new information.

What, we may further ask in that case, is being drawn out of the students? It is not so much something they possess in a rudimentary form as something deeper within the mind or character or personality. In short, the object of education is the mind of the student, and thereby his character and personality as well.

Here we come to the distinction that has often been drawn, at least since Newman proposed his *Idea of a University* in Dublin in the early 1850s, between a liberal and a utilitarian (or practical) education. Those were the days of the Industrial Revolution, when many new universities were being founded in the industrial towns of England. At such new universities, in contrast to Oxford and Cambridge, emphasis was placed on knowledge that would be useful for industry and for obtaining jobs in industries—that is to say, on scientific or technical knowledge.

Such an emphasis, however, overlooked the whole purpose of university education as it had been conceived until then. Such a utilitarian education might be appropriate for a scientific or research institute. Or it may more profitably be given to employees once they have entered a particular company. Indeed, all too often the education students have received in the science department of a university isn't quite what is required in such a company, and so the company finds it has to train its new members with a further, more-specialized kind of formation adapted to its special needs.

A liberal education, which means the education of a free man, is that education of the mind of which I have just been speaking. Specialized training for a trade or profession is, Newman held, an education of slaves in a servile state, while true education is the formation of a free man, or a gentleman, whose typical character he proceeds to define in one of the most famous passages in English prose.

> All that goes to constitute a gentleman—the
> carriage, gait, address, gestures, voice; the ease,
> the self-possession, the courtesy, the power of
> conversing, the talent of not offending; the lofty
> principle, the delicacy of thought, the happiness of
> expression, the taste and propriety, the generosity
> and forbearance, the candor and consideration, the
> openness of hand—these qualities, some of them
> come by nature, some of them may be found in
> any rank, some of them are a direct precept of
> Christianity; but the full assemblage of them,
> bound up in the unity of an individual character,
> do we expect they can be learned from books?
> Are they not necessarily acquired, where they are
> to be found, in high society?

To form such a free man, or rather the son or daughter
of such a free man, the imparting or eliciting of knowledge
is essential. As the food is to the body, so knowledge is to the

mind. By knowing all kinds of things—and not just things scattered here and there in confusion, but arranged in a due order—the human mind grows in stature. These things may be arranged in precise order, as in science, or in a free, personal order, as in literature. In either case they may be said to provide food for the mind.

"Man does not live by bread alone," said Jesus, quoting the words of Moses, "but by every word that proceeds from the mouth of God." That is so true of the inner spirit of man. But it may also be said, on a secular level, that man must live and grow to mental perfection through the words uttered by wise men both past and present.

We may, however, do well to remember that not every word uttered by a teacher, whether of science or literature, is wise or even factually true. Education, even when it is utilitarian, cannot consist merely of listening to what a teacher says, taking notes, and repeating it in an examination (according to the pattern observed in all too many universities). That is instruction for parrots, not human beings. Whatever the student hears in class has to be reflected upon and applied to himself. It may also need to be sifted in order to extract what is true and valuable from what is otherwise.

We have to bear in mind what the great Aristotle said of his teachers, for all their acknowledged greatness: "Plato is dear to me, but dearer to me is truth." Such is the truth that, according to Jesus, makes us free.

THREE

What Is Culture?

◆

A rt, architecture, sculpture, music, literature, drama, ballet, opera, and so on…In all these things we find the presence of what we call "culture." But what, we may ask, do they have in common to deserve the name of culture? We may think of another list—soccer, football, skiing, skating, gymnastics…Do we also find the presence of culture in these? Don't we rather think of them as sport, in contrast to culture? So what *is* culture?

It may be helpful to return to the original use of the word, which isn't so far back in time. The word acquired its modern meaning only about the middle of the nineteenth century. Before then, if we look for instance in the pages of

Dr. Samuel Johnson's great dictionary, first published in the middle of the eighteenth century, we find that *culture*, like the modern Italian *cultura*, is defined as "to till soil."

What on earth is there in common between the humble (from the Latin for "soil," *humus*) task of tilling the soil and the manifestations of human culture mentioned above? Evidently there is a perceived analogy between the lowly task of tilling the soil and the more exalted task of tilling the mind. For, in the development of language from concrete to abstract, we have to proceed by way of analogy.

In this abstract sense of tilling the mind we may recognize another way of defining *education*. As the farmer tills the soil to bring forth fruit for our bodily needs, so the teacher, whether at a university, a secondary school, or even a kindergarten, tills the soil of his students' minds so that they bring forth intellectual fruit in various forms, recognized as part of what we all call culture.

Genuine cultural manifestations aren't easy to produce without arduous training, which may well be compared to the labor of tilling the soil. One doesn't just sit down and write a symphony. Long training is needed and only practice makes perfect. This is true not only in the composition of original music, but also in the appreciation and performance of the work of others. And so it is with all the arts.

Now let me draw attention to a wider meaning of *culture* than is commonly implied in the various forms of art mentioned. When we speak, for example, of the culture of the Polynesians, we include almost every expression of art in their daily lives, however crude it may seem when judged by Western standards. So it seems that *culture* may be used to describe any manifestation of the human mind beyond the merely physical—as in fights or contests in which bodily strength and skill are tested.

In other words, such are the arts of peace as opposed to the arts of war, arts that are produced more abundantly and with greater skill in times of peace than in times of war. So we have the words of John Milton, "Peace hath her victories no less renowned than war."

I propose to hazard a theory about the origin of culture that has to do with the basic difference between man and woman. Although most of the great artists, architects, musicians, and poets of the past have been men—for various historical and social reasons, including the importance of childbearing and child rearing—culture comes primarily from women. Even when women have not produced the masterpieces of culture, in most cases I think they have inspired them.

There is an eternal contrast (and conflict) between the sexes, in spite of what feminists say with their insistence on equality—men have physical strength and women beauty and elegance of form. Men have the traditional function of guarding and protecting the family and providing food, whether meat from the chase or vegetables from the fields. For this they have need of physical strength. So it is natural for men to excel in sport and in war. To women, on the other hand, is assigned the no-less traditional function of looking after the growing family, preparing food, and weaving cloth for clothes. At this stage they have more time than their laboring husbands to elaborate on their cooking and weaving and so produce little works of culinary art and handicraft.

In such works of art we find a primitive culture in the sociological sense. Also, in the building and decorating of houses, men and women together unintentionally produce fine works of art. In such a situation it seems that everything they touch becomes a work of art and part of culture.

In my own experience, when arranging tours around England for my Japanese students, I have frequently had occasion to notice that almost everything produced before 1800, however humble, is a work of art, whereas what emerged from the dark smoke of the Industrial Revolution, however sophisticated, is ugly. In the Victorian age, for all its boasted accumulation of wealth arising from the British Empire, I find it difficult to point to anything of real cultural value, even if it comes from the hand of an acknowledged master.

Here I come to yet another distinction, that between culture and civilization. The former springs naturally from the hands of human beings living in society: it is an expression of their artistic minds, and it becomes increasingly sophisticated with the passing of time. It is often closely connected with religion as belief in God provides man with deep inspiration and the leisure to give artistic expression to that inspiration. The latter belongs to a later stage of human society, when men no longer live in families, clans, or tribes, but become submerged as citizens in a large impersonal state, such as that of Rome. Then, while the arts become more sophisticated, the religious inspiration behind human culture disappears in the process of secularization.

In either case it may be said that culture is the outcome of education; it is the tilling of the human mind in two successive stages. Of course, culture remains a part of civilization until the further stage of barbarian invasion sets in. And that is what seems to be happening today.

FOUR

What Is Religion?

◆

What has religion got to do with education? A great deal, I think, if not everything. The very posing of the question may be a sign that secularization has overtaken the West in the past two or three centuries.

As I have just shown, human culture may have its origin and inspiration in religion, in the worship of one God or many gods. Man is, it seems, most human when he comes closest to the divine. There is something about the human form, too, that has prompted such poets as Milton and Blake to speak with admiration of the human form divine.

Just as light comes down to earth from the sun, the moon, and the stars, and as water flows down from the mountains to human dwellings on the plains, so culture derives from religion.

The artifacts of human culture have their original place in daily life, in the building and decoration of houses, in the weaving of clothes. But objects of a more specifically artistic nature were commonly produced in the service of religion, for the worship of God. For this worship, certain days were set apart as holidays and festivals, when not only the priests, but also the people put on their best attire. The very word *holiday* means "holy day," and a festival was a feast in honor of a god or a saint.

Human learning may, in many cases, be traced to the sacred wisdom of priests, as in the religions of ancient Egypt and prehistoric Britain. The very idea of learning or lore was invested by common people with a religious halo. The word *grammar*, far from suggesting "dry as dust," has the same etymology as *glamour*.

In the West, where the institution of the university (as it has come down to us) had its origin in the thirteenth century, it was mainly the Christian clergy who were in charge of education. In those days, most clerics were scholars, and all scholars were clerics. Theology and education went hand in hand.

The first great university, that of Paris, has almost entirely disappeared. What is now called the Sorbonne has its roots in the secularization of the French Revolution. But in Oxford, one may still see what a medieval university was like. Almost all of its great colleges are medieval, going back (as in the case of Thomas Merton) even to the thirteenth century. What one notices about them is their monastic structure. Pride of place is accorded as much to the dining hall as to the college chapel (which is often hardly distinguishable on the outside from the dining hall).

One sees a profusion of Gothic pinnacles, not only on chapels and churches, but on other buildings as well, pointing insistently upward from earth to heaven. Here, it is implied, is the origin and end of all true human learning, the inspiration and fulfillment of human studies. In contrast, there is almost nothing to see in the Sorbonne, reconstructed as it has been according to the secular ideals of the French

Revolution. Visitors to Paris seldom go sightseeing to the Sorbonne, except perhaps occasionally for its connection with one of the famous modern scholars who have taught there. But everyone goes to the great cathedral of Notre Dame de Paris, where Gothic pinnacles soar heavenward as they did in medieval times.

Even in America, which shares much of the secular ideology of the French Revolution and has a much shorter history, many of the leading universities, such as Harvard, Princeton, and the University of Chicago, began as theological colleges or seminaries. Visiting their campuses, one notices—as opposed to the Sorbonne—the tapering white spires of university chapels.

Alas, when Japan was reopened to the West in the nineteenth century and set out to imitate Western institutions, including universities, the process of secularization had long since set in. The countries with which Japan now came into close contact in trade and culture, such as England, France, Germany, and the United States, were all traditionally Christian, but through secularization they kept their

Christianity out of sight. The Japanese imitated what they saw on the surface, neglecting what was hidden.

This secularization of culture is a strange phenomenon of the West, going back to the mid-seventeenth century. Curiously, one can date its origin precisely: it was a result of the Civil War (or Puritan rebellion) in England and the disastrous Thirty Years' War in Germany. Both wars had religious as well as political motives behind them, and once they were over the vexed issue of religion was replaced by the rising influence of science. It was seen as a more peaceful and practical option for the future of civilization.

What was less clearly realized, however, both then in Europe and today in Japan, is that true religion is a cause not of war, but of peace. The so-called wars of religion were waged as much for political as for religious reasons. Science, we have come to realize over the past two centuries, has come to serve the cause of war rather than peace, and on a scale undreamt of in past ages.

As that great historian of culture Christopher Dawson emphasized, it is from religion that both culture and civilization arose. The increasing sophistication of civilization leads to the connection between culture and religion being severed, and the outcome is the decline and decay of civilization. This decadence in the West has been highlighted by such eminent thinkers as Otto Spengler and T. S. Eliot.

FIVE

What Is Knowledge?

◆

A university, it is said, is a seat of learning. It has two main purposes with respect to learning: the transmission of knowledge to students and the extension of the frontiers of learning by means of research. Such a definition of the purpose of a university is today accepted by almost everyone; it is all but a cliché among scholars.

It is not for me to criticize, but perhaps one should ask, like the radical students at the time of the Berkeley Student Revolt, what is the point of it all? All too often academics seem to take refuge from the busy world around them and shut themselves up in impractical ivory towers. Even a great poet like William Wordsworth, who (unlike

William Shakespeare) had the benefit of a university education at Cambridge, complained, "Books! 'tis a dull and endless strife!" Then, as if addressing a typical dry-as-dust scholar, he went on, "Come forth into the light of things. Let Nature be your teacher."

To understand the point of it all, we have to go back to the beginning of human knowledge. This is to be found, as Aristotle observed, in wonder. "What is that?" asks a child, pointing to an animal. "That," you answer, "is a cow." And so the child is satisfied for a time. He has acquired a new piece of knowledge, even if it is only a name.

Everything we learn through our five senses begins with a feeling of wonder, not just at the name attached to it by a know-all adult, but also at the thing behind the name. All things, as things, are full of wonder, at least when we first come to know them. After a time we get used to them, and they no longer excite our wonder. So we turn to other things, moving as it were from wonder to wonder, until our very sense of wonder gets jaded. Then, as Wordsworth lamented, "shades of the prison-house" begin to close upon us, and the beauty and wonder of things "fade into the light of common day."

All knowledge, so long as it is a true knowledge of things, has this quality of wonder. A great scholar may be said to be one who keeps this quality alive in his heart; a great teacher is one who communicates it to his students.

Now where, I wonder, does this quality of wonder come from? Take the cow. First, the very existence of the cow is a matter for wonder. There it stands in a green field, with four legs supporting its unwieldy brown body and a squarish head from which emerge two horns. If one has never seen a cow before, it is an amazing animal. One just gazes and gazes on it, as Wordsworth once gazed on the daffodils. Naturally we come to take the animal for granted—so long as it remains on earth. If an astronaut were to encounter the cow on the moon, how astonished he would be! And how astonished we would be to read about it in the papers the next day!

Needless to say, if we retained this degree of wonder all the time there would be no advancement in knowledge. We would be content with what we knew already. Perhaps that is why there seems to have been so little advancement in knowledge for so many centuries, until the time of Sir Francis Bacon in the early seventeenth century, when he wrote a book with this very title. People had been content with what they knew while they remained close to things in the countryside, but by Bacon's time many of them had been herded out of the countryside into towns like London.

Learning may be said to have taken its rise from the invention of writing, many centuries before the appearance of the new science. Before then, men had to rely on memory in order to hand down the knowledge of previous generations. With written signs, such as we find in ancient China and Egypt, learning, as contrasted with knowledge, may be said to have come into existence. This was the beginning of what we call book learning, which became scholarly erudition.

Thus from the wonder of things one moves to the other wonder, or glamour, of words. But scholars tend to bury their heads in books, away from the cares of the world, becoming hermits of learning. It was to such bookworms that Wordsworth addressed his perhaps exasperated words,

"Books! 'tis a dull and endless strife…Come forth into the life of things!"

A further important stage in the history of learning came with the invention of movable type in the mid-fifteenth century, a full two centuries after the founding of the first European universities. Until then, all books had to be painstakingly copied, usually by monks in monasteries. Now they could be rapidly reproduced and circulated among many readers. This was an important factor in the dissemination of the new learning emanating from such scholars as Erasmus.

This new learning, however, shared the fate of all things new: it soon became old. Great scholars like Erasmus were all too soon replaced by the sort of schoolmasters and pedants satirized by Shakespeare in *Love's Labour's Lost*. It was against this background of decadent humanism that Bacon proposed his new method of learning, which was not so much literary as scientific. He laid emphasis, like Wordsworth, not on mere books, but on "the light of things," which constitute the book of Nature—which existed alongside the book of scripture.

Herein lies the basic distinction in all university learning between literature, human words set down in books, and science, the study of things seen in the world of nature. There is a further distinction, implied above, between the attitude of someone like Bacon, a prophet of the new science, and that of a poet like Wordsworth. The former seeks to explore the hidden secrets of nature; the latter is content to contemplate what he finds on the surface.

A further kind of wonder arises from the endeavor to put all these wonderful things (for the scientist) or words (for the humanist) together in new and different forms. Thus are the frontiers of knowledge, both scientific and literary, ever being pushed back. There does not seem to be any limit but the sky—and even the sky is no limit for astronomers.

SIX

What Is Wisdom?

◆

I have still a question about knowledge as food for the mind and as the means of education at a university. I still can't help asking myself, what is the point of it all? Is any kind of knowledge appropriate for the student, or an appropriate form of nourishment for his mind?

I can't help thinking of two learned friends of mine who did their doctoral theses, one at the University of Chicago, the other at Oxford. One took as his subject the molar teeth of the gibbon monkey. By the time he had finished his thesis, I am sure what he didn't know about the molar teeth of the gibbon monkey wasn't worth knowing. But it also occurred to me that what he did know might not be worth knowing either!

The other devoted his research to an obscure Arabic philosopher, Al Bhakilani. I remarked to him that he must have come to the conclusion that this thinker had been unduly neglected by historians of philosophy. "On the contrary," he responded, "I have reached the conclusion that Al Bhakilani is of no importance whatever!" Why then, I wondered, waste so much time and energy on him?

On this point I found myself opposed by no less an authority on university education than John Henry Newman, who proposed that knowledge is its own end, or an end in itself. What did he mean? And what light would that throw on the two instances I have just given of apparently useless knowledge?

Newman evidently meant that there is value in the knowledge of anything, both as it is knowledge and as it is directed to a thing—whether that thing be the molar teeth of a gibbon monkey or the philosophy of Al Bhakilani. There is nothing so mean or insignificant but has its own value. And in his study of those molar teeth, my friend must have gained a lot of other knowledge about the gibbon monkey and about monkeys in general—and no doubt about human beings as well. My other friend must have learned a lot about Arabic philosophy and acquired a good knowledge of the Arabic language and the Arabic world.

There is a big difference between this kind of knowledge, in which facts are organized in relation to a single end, no matter how insignificant it may seem, and the random knowledge picked up by students under the heading of general culture. That is the sort of knowledge one gets from reading general-interest magazines. It does not have the unity or order of the knowledge acquired by thesis writers. As the bits and pieces are unrelated to anything in particular, most of them are soon forgotten, leaving hardly a trace behind. What is the value of such knowledge?

I am leading up to a further point about university education that is specially emphasized by Newman. He sees knowledge as an end in itself, but he also looks to an end to knowledge that is more than knowledge. There are two ways of acquiring knowledge. One way is to pick up bits and pieces of information, which may be called indiscriminate or random knowledge, such as is acquired by perusing an encyclopedia. The other way is to relate such bits and pieces to each other so that they throw light on each other and on the world as a whole. This becomes what may be called "ordered knowledge." When the different parts are studied together and seen to support each other, they are less likely to be forgotten.

Such ordered knowledge comes close to the ideal of wisdom, which was for Newman the chief aim of a university education. In other words, there are two levels or layers to be distinguished in the acquiring of knowledge. The first is the mere accumulation of facts, as when students attend a lecture and take notes on what the lecturer says. He is instructing them, and they are learning from his instruction. The second level is when they go on to reflect on what he has said, comparing it with what they have read or what they are about to read, and find things coming together in a unity—which is what we mean by "understanding" or "comprehension." It may all come to them in the sudden light of discovery, and then they may exclaim, "I've got it!" or, as the ancient Greek shouted, "Eureka!"

This second level, properly called "understanding," is not yet wisdom. That further most precious stage comes when the student not merely comprehends what he has learned, whether from his teachers or his books, but makes it his own by recognizing its hidden value to his life and the world around him. That is wisdom, at least in the classical sense of the word.

But I now come to a further sense of wisdom that one finds not so much in the classical philosophy of Greece and Rome as in the sacred scriptures of Israel, the Bible. A certain question is repeated again and again in the so-called books of wisdom, the Psalms, Job, and the Proverbs: "Where is wisdom to be found?" The answer, if I may be allowed to give it at once, is that wisdom is to be found not in any scientific study of nature or humanist study of books, but in the fear of the Lord.

Here is where religion may be seen to have an important place in the education provided at a university.

It adds a wholly new dimension to human life. Without it, university studies would remain two-dimensional. Nature, the object of science, may be said to form one dimension, and books, the concern of literature, the other. The third and most important dimension, almost universally neglected in modern universities, is the divine dimension that teaches us all that is true in the words of man and all that is good in the works of nature.

Thus, as all knowledge comes from and leads to a sense of wonder. In that wonder we feel ourselves in the unseen presence of God.

SEVEN

What Is Philosophy?

◆

C losely connected with the ideal of wisdom as the end of university education is the subject of philosophy. The word *philosophy* (from the Greek) originally meant "love of wisdom" and it is said to go back to the old Greek philosopher Pythagoras, who modestly disclaimed the appellation of "wise man," averring that he was only a lover of wisdom.

In the Middle Ages, when so many of the great European universities were founded, philosophy had pride of place, subject only to theology, as queen of the sciences. Alas, theology is now largely neglected and philosophy has been relegated to a lowly position as handmaiden to science. Even at Oxford, the principal function of philosophy, apart from the study of its history, is seen as the useful way in which it clarifies terms used in science. Already in the eighteenth century, Alexander Pope lamented in his *Dunciad*:

> Philosophy, that leaned on heaven before,
> Shrinks to her second cause, and is no more.
> Physic of Metaphysic begs defence,
> And Metaphysic calls for aid on sense!

All too often in modern universities, the department of philosophy is mainly devoted to the exposition of the ideas of great philosophers of old, from ancient Greece to contemporary Europe and America. And all too often such exposition seems difficult and remote from the real problems of human life. This is true of modern as well as ancient philosophy. Or rather, ancient philosophy as expressed in the words of Socrates is a good deal easier to understand than the verbiage of modern philosophers, especially those of the German schools, from Kant and Hegel to Heidegger.

Yet I cannot see why philosophy should be regarded as difficult. It ought to be the simplest of all the subjects studied at a university. It is indeed capable of being so simple that I suspect many modern philosophers and professors of philosophy deliberately conceal its simplicity beneath a mask of complexity in order to create a false impression of profundity. If they were to present their ideas simply, their listeners would conclude they had nothing of importance to say—as indeed they don't.

Not that I wish to be uncharitable. A reason for their difficulty is that they have read too many books of philosophy, explaining too many different schools of thought throughout the ages. They have become accustomed to reading difficult books, so when they go on to write their own they can't avoid similar forms of expression. Perhaps they fear being ignored or despised by their peers and students.

Thinking about such books of philosophy, I again sympathize with Wordsworth. "Books! 'tis a dull and endless strife!" I feel like saying to such philosophers and professors of philosophy, "Come forth into the light of things!" Philosophy, as queen of the sciences, should depend not on books, but on the light of nature.

Take, for example, any one of those difficult words with which philosophy has been associated for centuries, especially since scholars of the Middle Ages began the tedious task of commenting on the writings of Aristotle. Take a word like *metaphysics*. It's enough to scare any student at first sight. All it means in the original Greek is "the study that comes after that of nature"—*meta* is Greek for "after" or "beyond," *physis* is "nature." That is all. It is the word used by Aristotle for his discussion of matters implicit in his previous study of natural causes in *The Physics*. In his explanation it is simple enough.

Or take the name of the related science of ontology. Like so many philosophical terms, it comes from Greek: *on* for "being" and *logos* for "word"—the word that provides the suffix in the names of most sciences. In other words, ontology is the science of being, or that which is inasmuch as it is. But what can be said of being except that it is? Or rather, how can it be said of being that it is? Isn't it just an abstract concept (if it can be called a concept) for concrete things inasmuch as they are? Surely, the more one withdraws from concrete things into a world of abstractions, the further one gets away from being? Being in itself is the most abstract of all abstractions, the least true to itself. So one gets involved in the contradiction and confusion that is typical of philosophy.

But now I myself seem to have got involved, for all my protests about its simplicity, in the complicated world of philosophy. But is it so difficult? Haven't I overcomplicated it by taking certain philosophical terms and trying to explain them in the light of their etymological origins? Although there is nothing difficult in this, it may lead, as I have shown, to seeming contradiction.

In speaking of being, one should be dealing not with the abstract concept, whatever that may be, but with the actual things that are and that may be said to participate in being. Being isn't so much a concept as a word that refers not to ideas or qualities in things, but to the fact that they exist. They are. It echoes the insistence of the old Greek philosopher Parmenides, "That that is is"—and "that that is not is not." There is surely nothing difficult about his words, to which I have added the negative parallel; in fact, it seems too obvious to be worth saying.

One reason why Christian philosophers in medieval and modern times have laid such emphasis on being is, I think, because it is strangely related to the name of God as revealed to Moses in the Old Testament. When Moses asked God to tell him his name, God replied, "I am who am" (or "I am who I am"). This is commonly taken to mean that while creatures only have being in one particular form, only of God can it be said that he is being. He is the being in all things, that by which they are what they are, while he remains in himself, within and above them all.

Thus the more one reflects on the things around oneself, and on oneself amid those things, the more one is led into the presence of one who is far greater—insofar as one can compare him with anything outside himself—within them all and above them all. And so from philosophy, especially from the philosophy of being, one passes almost without realizing it to theology—as Aristotle himself realized when he called metaphysics a kind of theology.

This natural transition is, however, forbidden in modern academic thought, with all its absurd prejudices. It insists on maintaining an artificial separation of theology from philosophy, as of church from state (and originally of God from man). Such a separation stands in the way of true philosophy, which should, as their queen and sovereign mistress, rise above divisions in the sciences.

EIGHT

What Is Science?

◆

The original meaning of *science*, from the Latin *scientia*, was simply "knowledge." It stood for the whole object of university education. It is by knowledge both of himself and of the world around him that a student is educated at school, and especially at university. Thus he comes to that knowledge of the truth that, as Jesus says, makes him truly free.

From the foundation of the first universities in the thirteenth century, this object of knowledge included not only what we now call science, but also, and especially, philosophy—leading up to the three professional subjects, theology, law, and medicine. As I have said, the relationship that existed then between philosophy and science is the opposite of what prevails today. We have now come to think of philosophy as a special kind of learning on the fringes of science—or even of literature. Before it was science that was relegated to the inferior regions of philosophy.

In the Middle Ages, when they spoke simply of "the philosopher" they meant Aristotle. It was he who provided the universities with their basic textbooks of philosophy and science. They might equally have spoken of him as "the scientist." His books covered most of human knowledge: the world of nature, the use of words, the soul of man, and the ideals of morality, of politics, of poetry, and of society.

Of all his books, the one that comes closest to what we think of as science is *Physics*. Today there is an immense proliferation of divisions and subdivisions within science, physics being but one, admittedly important, part. It is even divided from chemistry, electricity, and mathematics under the more general heading of science. But for Aristotle, and up until the eighteenth century, physics was physical science, the philosophy of nature.

The primary object of science, in its original meaning,

was to investigate the world of nature that surrounds us. It studied the nature of everything it found—for nature or *natura* is in Latin what physics or *physis* is in Greek. *Natura* is literally what a thing is born to be, from the verb *nasci*, "to be born"; *physis* comes from the verb *phyein*, meaning "to grow."

The original concerns of physical science, therefore, were not so much everything outside ourselves in the visible world as *all* living things—plants, animals, and even human beings. The whole philosophy of Aristotle was concerned with living things, especially the phenomena of life, birth and growth, and then decay and death. He noted how plants and animals come from particular seeds, with distinct powers or potentialities, and how in the course of time they grew to the fullness of their nature, or what he called "fullness in act." This spirit of wonder at the phenomena of life produced the seed that blossomed into his own living philosophy. Alas, it has been deadened by generations of dull philosophers.

Such was the physical or natural philosophy inherited by the prophets of the new science, Bacon and Galileo, at the beginning of the seventeenth century. However, instead of reflecting with childlike wonder on the nature of living things, the new scientists proceeded to measure and analyze objects in the outside world, animate or inanimate. Aristotle had progressed from his study of the world of nature in *Physics* to the study of philosophy in *Metaphysics*. The new scientists, in contrast, limited their attention to the visible material world, progressing from unity to variety, from one unified knowledge to unending divisions and subdivisions. As Milton remarked of the academic devils in hell, they "found no end, in wandering mazes lost."

The very words *physic* and *physical* have come to have two very different meanings. In the science of physics, the emphasis is on matter rather than life. Scientists involved in this are called "physicists." On the other hand, we have *physic*, meaning "medicine." The doctors who prescribe it are called "physicians" since the medicines originally used were derived (as Friar Laurence in *Romeo and Juliet* tells us) from the hidden powers in herbs or other plants.

In the development of science we may observe an

interesting paradox. Whereas it began with the world of nature, plants, and animals, it has become increasingly removed from nature. The analysis to which it subjects things is conducted not in the outside world of nature, but in artificial conditions within a laboratory. It is no longer concerned with living things, reducing them instead, for purposes of laboratory analysis, to inanimate matter.

There is, it is true, something impressive about the progress of knowledge (as Bacon hailed it), both in itself and in its various applications to modern life and industry. We now know the world and its resources in ways undreamt of before the seventeenth century. We sometimes wonder how human beings could have lived or done what they did without the benefits of modern science. My students are amazed at how the great cathedrals of the Middle Ages could have been built without the sophisticated technology provided by modern science.

But there is also something disturbing about the way we have been cut off by technological advances from the world of nature. We have come to rely too much on modern machinery and technology—as we realize all too well during a brief power outage. What would happen if we were deprived of electricity for weeks? What would become of us? And then there is something even more terrifying: our possession of atomic power.

NINE

What Is Literature?

◆

In the medieval university, pride of place was accorded to theology—or, as it was then called in English, divinity. Second to theology came philosophy, especially that branch of philosophy known as ontology, the science of being. Among the lesser forms of philosophy was, as we have seen, the philosophy of nature, which developed in part into physical science. Scholars or students of theology were known as divines, those of natural philosophy naturalists.

Then what place had literature in the university curriculum? Alas, a very inferior one. It was not regarded as a science or branch of knowledge, but as an art, namely the art of writing. That is why the degree for literature (and other subjects too) came to be known as a BA or bachelor of arts, but without a corresponding degree of DA or doctor of arts. The further degree for literature students is doctor of philosophy, though these further studies may have little to do with philosophy as such.

Things changed with the arrival of the new learning advocated by the humanists, such as Erasmus, in the early sixteenth century. The very appellation "humanist" implies that they were students of the humanities, the classical literature of Greece and Rome. Latin literature had been studied throughout the Middle Ages, if only as a preparation for other, more important studies. From the fourteenth century onward, the study of Greek was also introduced, especially in Italy. From then on, Latin and Greek together formed the basis of what came to be called a classical education. The more recent literatures of other countries were almost entirely ignored as unfit objects of study.

Such was the liberal education, the education for free men, that Newman chiefly had in mind. He had learned it in his student days at Oxford and wished to apply it to the new Catholic university in Dublin, as shown in his lectures on *The Idea of a University*, one of which is devoted to the subject of literature. Such was still the education I received at secondary school and Oxford University, though by then it was losing ground to science. In society at large the liberal ideal was giving way to utilitarian considerations.

So what is meant by "literature" as a university subject—that is, as a branch of knowledge? And how is it to be taught at university, in contrast to science?

The word *literature* actually includes everything that is written down in words. Language began with spoken words, but once letters were invented it came to be written down, with greater or less skill. There are all kinds of written documents—laws, medical prescriptions, treatises on philosophy and science (such as those of Aristotle)... But they are not usually what we mean by literature, unless they are written with attention to style. So, while Aristotle's treatises (which were little more than his lecture notes) are not so literary, even when he was writing on literature in *Poetics*, the dialogues of Plato have a distinguished place in the history of literature as well as of philosophy.

In early literature almost anything written down with some attention to style is accepted among the literary remains of that language. But in the course of time, especially with the introduction of printing in the fifteenth century and the subsequent proliferation of printed books from the sixteenth century onward, a distinction came to be made between writings of greater and lesser quality. In content, literature came to be limited to poetry, drama, and prose stories or novels, as well as essays of various kinds, to the gradual exclusion of history and devotional works.

Thus, whereas in science emphasis is laid on analytical reasoning, observing, measuring, calculating, and drawing conclusions, in literature it is laid rather on the creative imagination. This is the distinction notably drawn by Newman in his lecture on literature. "Science," he observes, "has to do with things, literature with thoughts; science is universal, literature is personal; science uses words merely as symbols, but literature uses language in its full compass, as including phraseology, idiom, style, composition, rhythm, eloquence, and whatever other properties are included in it."

Not that there is no room for reason in literature, as originally written or as studied, but reason has to go together with the imagination. Neither does literature avoid what is universal, but it combines what is universal with what is personal. Science, as we commonly think of it, may exclude a personal use of imagination in objective analysis, but literature excludes nothing. All things may be taken up and processed by the creative imagination.

Science may thrive on division—what is called "departmentalization"—but not a few scientists are now having second thoughts about what looks like a cancerous proliferation in the body of human knowledge. Literature knows no such division—not even a separation from philosophy or religion—though some literary scholars may allow their own prejudices to erect a division, especially from religion. The humanist motto is that of the Latin dramatist Terence: "I am a man, and nothing that is human I regard as alien to me."

In speaking of literature, one has to note the difference

between original writing and its subsequent study. The great writers of the past were not, of course, writing in or for a university. They were for the most part living and writing in and for the outside world. But in a university one may well study their writings, not only for literary enjoyment (as could any reader, student or not), but also to analyze their style, their use of words, and their understanding and representation of human nature and individual human beings. And one may also be encouraged to go and do likewise, to produce one's own works of literary merit and creative imagination.

In this way the study of literature, whether within or outside the university, may be both a science and an art. It may be called a science for its analysis of literary works and its study of them in their historical context. And it may also be called an art for its appreciation of those works and the practical application of them to the composing of further works, whether poems or essays, plays or novels.

TEN

What Is Language?

◆

U p until fairly recent times, no distinction was made between the study of literature and the study of language, at least at university level. The main difference between the two is in the obvious meaning of the words. Language is what one speaks with the tongue (*lingua* in Latin); literature is its written form, using letters (*litterae* in Latin).

There is a further difference between writing that reflects the ordinary speech of the writer and an artificial style that elaborates on ordinary speech. Such a style commonly reflects the influence of a classical, especially Latin, education. The great model for fine writing was formerly Cicero, who used what is called a periodic style in carefully balanced periods or sentences. His style is called golden, in contrast to the silver or more terse and pointed style of Tacitus and Seneca, who appeared in the following generation.

In English literary style we don't usually employ special words or special grammatical forms. We mostly rely on ordinary words, but in more elaborate sentences than we would use in ordinary conversation. In the history of English prose, there are periods when, owing to the influence of Puritanism, or of science, or of democracy (as in the late seventeenth century), a simpler style closer to common speech was preferred to a more elaborate one.

Here is an important difference between the humanism of the Renaissance and the rise of the new science in the following century. In the modern mind these two movements are commonly confused, as two stages in the same reaction to the culture, or lack of it, of the Middle Ages. But whereas humanism was essentially a literary movement, with the emphasis on Ciceronian style, the rise of science was in no small measure a reaction against the addiction to fine words and phrases, in favor of simplicity in words and thoughts.

To return to the distinction between language as spoken and literature as written, until recently it was generally considered in Europe that there is no place for the teaching of language at university level. Such teaching was thought to belong to secondary schools or special language colleges, not to universities. Those wishing to specialize in English or French or German or the classics were assumed already to have a mastery of the language in question.

If I may now speak of my own experience in Japan, I was surprised when I came to Tokyo from Oxford and found whole universities devoted to the study of languages. At my own university there is a faculty of literature, including a Department of English Literature, and a separate faculty of foreign languages, including a Department of English Language. Of these two English departments, the latter, although the more recent, is the larger and more popular. Students wish to attain proficiency in spoken English rather than in the literature of my country.

In such a preference, I see two basic misconceptions

about English. The first is that my Japanese students think that English literature shares the peculiarly literary style used in Japanese literature. They fail to see how a study of English literature can help them learn good spoken English. In my English boyhood it was through the study of French literature that we came to some mastery of the French language, to be improved, no doubt, by traveling to France. In prewar Japan, before the introduction of linguistics from the United States, it was through the study of English literature that Japanese students came to acquire a mastery of the English language— and a better mastery than they have today.

The second misconception is that English literature, especially poetry, has to be studied through the eye, with attention to vocabulary and frequent reference to the dictionary. But in fact, English prose, and especially poetry, have to be read as much with the ear as with the eye. In English literature, even when written in an elaborate Ciceronian style, the sentences are meant to be heard as well as read. Writing always presupposes speaking. In poetry, if the reader fails to hear the rhythm of the words, their assonance and alliteration as well as the rhymes, he will lose much of the poetic effect.

There is also a third misconception, affecting not so much the study as the teaching of English literature in Japan, and that is the excessive reliance on the method of translation in class. It is as if the Department of English Literature is regarded as a kind of school for translators, just as the Department of English Language is regarded as a kind of language school. No doubt when I was at school our study of the classics took the form of translation from Greek or Latin into English, and of prose composition from passages of English into Latin or Greek, but at university we paid more attention to the literary qualities of the authors we studied and read their writings more sensitively.

Because of this way of thinking in Japan and elsewhere in the world today, too much emphasis is laid on practical or useful English, on language patterns, idioms, and vocabulary. Long passages of trivial conversation are committed to memory, as if this will be of any help in a real-life situation. It is not only useless, it is harmful. If students are to memorize English words—which is certainly to be recommended—they should rather learn poetry by heart. Poems may not seem so practical—people don't speak in poetic language—but they are easier to memorize than prose, however conversational. By learning such poems, the students will be acquiring English in much the same way as native speakers of English do. They may not have occasion to quote the poems in ordinary conversation, but they will become accustomed to the words and rhythms of the English language. What is more, they will obtain a precious key to the mentality and the culture of the English people.

ELEVEN

What Is Art?

◆

If the object of a university education is knowledge—science in the wider meaning of the word—it seems there should be no place for the teaching of either literature or language, let alone what we nowadays mean by "art." When I came to Japan, I felt that there was a contradiction in the presence in universities not only of the study of foreign languages, but also of the study of the various arts, including music. It is good for such arts to be studied and practiced, but not at a university.

Here I am speaking of university in the original, medieval sense of the word, as an institution for the study of universal knowledge. Such knowledge is essentially theoretical. What we learn of scientific theory may later be applied to some form of industry, but industry as such has no place on the campus of a university.

On the other hand, when we speak of literature as an art, according to medieval usage, there is a certain ambiguity in the word. What comes first is the study of literature, usually the great masterpieces of the past, the classics, whether of Greece or Rome or of England. Such study, as in the case of science, gives rise to knowledge. One could even speak of a science of literature. But with literature, the more we read the great masterpieces of the past, the more we feel impelled to imitate them in our own way. That is where knowledge, which is theoretical, gives place to art, which is practical.

It was in this way that the movement of humanism in the early sixteenth century, though almost exclusively concerned with the classics of Greek and Latin, gave rise to a new literature and drama in the latter half of that century, not just in England, but in most European countries. The humanists themselves were not concerned about writing in the vernacular, which many of them despised, but the study of Greek and Latin literature prompted students to respond to the needs of their own age by writing poems, plays, and stories in their own language, for their fellow countrymen.

The same is true of the other arts—painting, music; sculpture, architecture, and so on. One begins by studying the great masterpieces of the past, not only showing aesthetic appreciation, but also paying attention to the artistic method employed in them. A knowledge of those masterpieces might only produce a feeling of awe, without any impulse toward imitation, but studying their artistic method kindles the impulse to do something similar, if not so great. After all, even the masters had to begin somewhere. They did not achieve perfection all at once.

Thus it may be said of every art that it includes two aspects—theoretical knowledge, which belongs to university education, and practical creation, which looks from the campus to the *atelier*, the *conservatoire*, or the studio.

There is something else of great importance to be said about the place of the arts, including literature, in a university. Whereas we see the sciences proceeding by way of division and subdivision in unending departmentalization, we find the arts, as they develop over the ages, assisting and illustrating one another. For example, the more we know about literature and drama, painting and music and religion in the Elizabethan age, the age of Shakespeare, the more we find them throwing light on each other. From the study of each art we come to a deeper understanding of the age and the culture in which it was created, not to mention a deeper understanding of the individual artist.

Here is a kind of knowledge different from that of science, which looks to the nature of things apart from their historical context. Through the study of art and literature we may come to a deeper understanding of history, perhaps better than that of a professional historian who pays more attention to political events and the important persons involved in those events. Through the study of art and literature, both particular masterpieces and general methods, we may be able to trace a history of human culture and the successive manifestations of the spirit of man.

Here, too, we see the contrast between science,

the knowledge of nature in the outside world, and art, the knowledge of man in his own world. Not only literature, but all forms of art reflect what Shakespeare called the "little world of man." From what is merely on the material surface of things, to which the new science sadly chose to restrict its view, we turn to what is at the heart of man and nature. As Gerard Manley Hopkins reflected, "And what is Earth's eye, tongue, or heart else, where else, but in dear and dogged man?"

In its excessive attention to the outward, measurable, and calculable forms of things, and with its concern for objective knowledge, the new science from the time of Bacon abandoned the aim of the older philosophy to enter into the heart of man. But this is an aim pursued by the arts, and most of all by the great masterpieces of literature that recur from age to age, though perhaps less frequently and less obviously in the modern age.

Newman, who in his *Idea of a University* laid as much emphasis on literature as on science in university education, allowed little room for the other arts. But well before he died, one of his successors at Oxford, Walter Pater, emphasized the importance of a knowledge of the arts in university education. It was also Pater who, with Matthew Arnold, did much to develop the ideas of culture in general and the Renaissance in particular. To the names of those Oxford men may be added a third, that of John Ruskin, who became the first Slade Professor of Art at Oxford University.

Thus we see how, in the context of a venerable medieval university, there may take place a harmonious development from the ideal of knowledge to that of art, even in the special sense of the latter term.

TWELVE

What Is Nature?

◆

One of the key words in university education, yet a bewilderingly ambiguous one, is *nature*. On the one hand, it describes the object of scientific study as opposed to the human subject engaged in that study—the world of nature in contrast to man and civilization. On the other hand, man also belongs to the world of nature. We speak of human nature as well as the nature of plants and animals.

The new science, with its emphasis on objectivity, came to include matter in its study of nature. Paradoxically, it became further and further removed from the natural world and involved in a world of artifice. At the same time, literature moved from a concentration on man, in the humanist age of the Renaissance, to an increasing preoccupation with the world of nature, the world of living things around us—not so much in the city as in the countryside. William Wordsworth was the self-styled priest and prophet of nature in the Romantic age.

This change from science to literature, from man to nature, happens as science and technology begin to appear enemies of nature. The industrial age has created machines that have given man superhuman powers, enabling him to build mammoth cities like London, New York, and Tokyo, which have destroyed the surrounding countryside. It is a new manifestation of the knowledge of good and evil that tempted Adam and Eve in Paradise. The story of Adam and Eve, as we read it in the book of Genesis, refers to every age in the history of man, and not least to our modern age.

Yet another meaning of nature is seen in its contrast to art—not only in the contrast between science and literature, inasmuch as the former is said to look to nature while the latter is called art, but within literature itself. Here nature, whether in man himself or in the outside world, is seen as a source of inspiration to writers. They are urged by Alexander Pope to "follow nature." Art is said to consist in the rules devised by human reason, if on the basis of nature. Nature is seen as more profound than reason, just as the outside world is wider and deeper than man. In this context we find art and reason paradoxically associated with the new science in the Age of Reason, the eighteenth century, while nature and the imagination are more closely connected with literature in the Romantic age. The two sides have surreptitiously changed places! Nature is increasingly championed by poets but undermined by science.

There remains a further meaning of *nature* that refers to the fallen nature of man in contrast to the redeeming grace of God. This is a theological distinction. Christian theology distinguishes three stages in human development. First comes the original nature of man, in his state of innocence, before the fall. Next comes fallen human nature when, as Saint Paul lamented, "The good that I would I do not, but the evil that I would not I do." Lastly, there is the redemption of man by the grace of God through Jesus Christ. This distinction is by no means limited to theology. It has a pervasive influence on English literature, which is a deeply Christian literature.

In Shakespeare's tragedy *King Lear*, this contrast is implicit throughout the play. Lear is not just a foolish old man betrayed by his anger into an act of injustice against Cordelia, his one faithful daughter; he is also Everyman. His folly in banishing the good Cordelia is intended to echo the sin of man in choosing the knowledge of good and evil rather than the grace of God. She is described as the "one daughter, who redeems nature from the general curse" and as returning from exile to save her father. This play is fully in the medieval tradition of morality plays such as *Everyman*, though by the time of Shakespeare that tradition had for various reasons gone, as we might say, underground.

The Biblical tradition is openly revealed by John Milton, the Puritan poet, in *Paradise Lost*. This is about the original nature of Adam before the fall, his descent into sin with Eve, and his promised redemption through Jesus Christ.

Turning from literature to the other arts, who does not see how important nature is to them, in every sense of the word? The history of art over the past four centuries is revealing. The central place in Renaissance art is occupied by man; the world of nature provides little more than a lovely landscape background. By the mid-seventeenth century the central place is occupied by nature, especially in the form of landscapes and still-life paintings. In modern times, there has been in all the arts a strange turning away from both man and nature toward abstract forms that defy interpretation. How may one find in them the ideal of nature? And, if we cannot, how can they rightly be called art?

This is a question that has to be answered not by modern artists, who are too involved in their own art to view it impartially, but by those viewing the whole history of culture as it has come down to us from ancient times. Particularly in Western culture we notice how closely religion was wedded to every form of culture, art, literature, and philosophy throughout the Middle Ages and the Renaissance. But then, with the wars of religion and the rise of science in the seventeenth century, there came a strangely sudden secularization of culture—as it were, in Shakespeare's words, "a second fall of cursed man." Since that time, Western culture has become increasingly cut off from its religious roots. We can hold the rise of science responsible not only for the industrial revolution in the nineteenth century, but also for two world wars within living memory. During this period I can't help noting a parallel decay in literature and the arts.

THIRTEEN

What Is Law?

◆

In almost all universities, in Japan as well as in the West, in the Middle Ages as well as today, pride of place has been accorded to the faculty or school of law. Other faculties and departments change from age to age, but that of law remains, basic as it is to human society.

Today we think chiefly of civil law, the law of the country in which we live as citizens. Within this law there may be various divisions, such as constitutional and criminal law, but beyond it we see nothing. In the Middle Ages, when the church maintained a presence parallel to the state, canon law, the law of the church, existed alongside civil law, the law of the state.

The law of the church and that of the state are termed "positive law," which is decreed by lawfully appointed legislators. We commonly take it for granted that such law is, on the whole, good for us and good for the country, and so we obey it. But such an attitude of easy compliance with the law is not necessarily a good one. Not all laws are good. Not all legislators are wise. It may be necessary to take a stand against a particular law, if we have firm grounds for regarding it as unjust.

We may at least demand to know on what grounds legislators have made certain laws or determined the basic constitution of the country. We expect legislators to have followed their reason in the drafting of wise laws, and that their reason, limited though it be, will have followed the ideal of nature. So we return to the ideal of nature, meaning unfallen human nature. But since the fall of man that nature is all too easily swayed by passion and self-interest away from the common good—not least in our legislators, those same politicians whom we see in the media corrupted by bribes. Can we trust them to make wise laws?

We have to look from the fallen nature of man to an ideal of nature, or what is called the natural law. This is not what scientists mean by a law of nature, such as the laws of gravity or relativity, which refer to a certain order and pattern in the material world. Rather it is a term used by medieval theologians such as Thomas Aquinas, whose thought was still being reflected in *The Laws* of the Elizabethan theologian Richard Hooker in the time of Shakespeare. It may also be recognized in the ideal of the Tao (the Way) in Chinese and Japanese philosophy.

In other words, if we use our human reason in the right way, without being swayed by passion or self-interest, we should be able to discern what is morally good for us and what is morally wrong. Parents are always telling their children "Do this!" and "Don't do that!" These are not just arbitrary commands to limit the freedom of their offspring. As mature adults, they can see what is for their children's good. As the children grow up and come to the full use of reason, they no longer need their parents to tell them what is good or bad for them, or what is right and wrong. If they have been well brought up they will be able to see it for themselves, using their moral reason or conscience. What individuals need to do for themselves the legislative assembly must do for the whole country.

Such is the way of nature, a way implicit in the natural world around us, as created by God and comprehended by us with the gift of reason. We may agree with particular laws made by the legislators of our country, or we may disagree with them even when they were using their collective reason. In most cases we have no choice but to obey the laws or be penalized, but where important moral issues are concerned we may be bound to disobey them and follow our own conscience. Sir Thomas More refused to obey his royal master King Henry VIII, even at the cost of losing his head.

In this way we pass from the field of law, as concerned with civil law, to the natural law, which comes under the scope of philosophy. And so we raise our eyes, with medieval philosophers and theologians and English poets, "from nature to nature's God." We also look from the natural law, or law of human nature, to the eternal law that is seen as dwelling in the mind of God from all eternity. Here we recognize the true basis of all just laws, in him whom we call the rock of ages. And here is also the true basis for our refusal to obey unjust laws, even if we have to suffer death in consequence. We may echo the words of Saint Peter to his Jewish judges: "Should we obey you rather than God?"

This study of law in its various degrees, from positive through natural to eternal, ought to have a central place in every university, even where there is no faculty of law. Such a faculty is naturally expected to go deeply into every aspect of positive law, far beyond the knowledge and understanding of most citizens. But when we raise our minds to the intrinsic nature and basis of law, that is a subject for philosophy, not for the science of jurisprudence.

Eternal law seems to be beyond our human understanding, but it is set out for Christians in the pages of the Bible. Here, too, distinctions have to be made. The law proposed by Moses on Mount Sinai was set aside in certain details by Jesus in his Sermon on the Mount. Jesus was looking away from some of the observances insisted upon by the scribes and Pharisees to the spirit of the law in the mind of his eternal Father—a spirit expressed in the twofold commandment to love God above all things and one's neighbor as oneself. This ideal of the law is indicated in the question, where is wisdom to be found? The answer points to "the fear of the Lord" as "the beginning of wisdom."

All this has meaning, it must be emphasized, not just for Christians, who accept the Bible as the word of God, but for everyone who can read the Bible and profit from it, as from any good book. It may also be accorded a place in any university curriculum, whether the university is Christian or not—without contravening the commonly misunderstood constitutional separation of church and state.

FOURTEEN

What Is Music?

◆

What is the place of music in university education?
Is music a form of knowledge? Indeed it is. There
are more forms of knowledge than can be expressed in
words. To adapt Hamlet's words, "There are more things in
heaven and earth"…than are dreamt of in most philosophies
of education. And there are more ways of expressing those
things than in words arising from human reason.

"Words move, music moves, only in time," said T. S.
Eliot. "Words, after speech, reach into the silence." In that
silence one may recognize an even greater music, the end
to which all human language, all human music, unutterably
tends. As Eliot also said, the aim of poetry is to achieve the

effect of music, and that effect is achieved, above all, in the silence that follows both forms of expression.

Music may be said to attend both the beginning and the end of human achievement. "From thee is my beginning, and for thee I end," sang the Roman poet Virgil in honor of his god Apollo. The same thought was put in a Christian form by the English poet Gerard Manley Hopkins, "Thee, God, I come from, to thee go."

So we have the ancient idea of the music of the spheres, that the planets in their courses produce an ideal music out of which all things in nature come into an orderly existence. "From harmony, from heavenly harmony," John Dryden sang in his "Song for St. Cecilia's Day," "this universal frame began...from harmony to harmony through all the compass of the notes it ran, the diapason closing full in man."

After all, the gift of reason, expressed in the words of human philosophy and science, isn't everything. There is also the gift of imagination, as expressed in human literature, both poetry and prose. And to these may be added the gift of inspiration, expressed not so much in words—though words may be added—as in music, which in turn reaches into a mystical silence.

"Here will we sit," said Shakespeare in the musical climax to *The Merchant of Venice*, "and let the sounds of music creep in our ears. Soft stillness and the night become the touches of sweet harmony." The nighttime setting of this scene, under the light of the myriad stars in the sky, is appropriate to sweet music, just as the light of the sun by day is right for the words of human reason in rational discourse.

In Greek mythology, the god of the sun was Phoebus Apollo, the patron of the nine Muses, whose shrine was at Delphi with the oracle. The goddess of the moon was his sister Phoebe, otherwise known as Diana, whose shrine was at Ephesus. Perhaps it was because the ancient Greeks saw something masculine in the light of day, the time for work and for rational discourse, and something feminine in the darkness of night, with the softer light of the stars, the time for rest and mystical contemplation.

In Christian theology, based on the Bible, the world is seen as having been created in six successive days—starting with the creation of light on the first day and ending with that of man on the sixth—by the creative Word of God. But before any word is uttered, there appears the divine Spirit moving over the face of the waters, and this Spirit again comes to rule over the divine rest on the seventh day. Thus, if the Word is seen as corresponding to the masculine power of reason in man, the Spirit may be seen as corresponding to the feminine ideal of music.

These two traditions of Greek mythology and Christian theology are basic to Christian culture. The Hellenic and the Hebraic (in Matthew Arnold's terms) are related to each other. In Oriental thought, originating in China, there is a similar pair of contrasting principles, yin and yang, the latter being the masculine principle of light, the former the feminine principle of darkness, if under the light of the moon and the stars.

The idea of such a contrasting but complementary pair, so deeply ingrained in human philosophy and religion, should not be confused with the Manichaean dualism of good and evil, the idea of two rival gods perpetually at strife with each other without beginning or end. Just as Shakespeare's duke in *As You Like It* learns to see "tongues in trees, books in the running brooks, sermons in stones," so does he also come to find "good in everything." Just as there is good in the light of day, so is there also another good in the dimly lit night. There is good in man, but so is there another good in woman.

Here is a deep truth in human life that we are in danger of overlooking today, with the spread of a male-oriented education and the rise of an argumentative feminism. It is the truth not only of a rational equality, but also of a natural difference between man and woman. Today's excessive emphasis on a rational, political, social, and legal equality between the sexes tends to blur their deeper distinction, rooted not only in the bodily functions of reproduction, but also in the psychology and inner spirit of man and woman.

In the long history of Western education, from primary school to university, pride of place has until very recently been accorded to men. This is due not just to male domination (or usurpation). The kind of education given in schools has been directed toward preparing men for their various tasks in the marketplace, whether of church or state. Women were thought to have no need of such education as their primary concern was with the home—which is by no means inferior to the marketplace.

Now that women are entering society in different ways and being educated alongside men, it has become necessary for the very nature of education to change. Women call for a greater emphasis on the imagination (as fostered by the study of literature) than on reason (as fostered by the study of science), and above all on the sweet "sound of music," moving from words to silence. So now I may add with Hamlet, "the rest is silence."

FIFTEEN

What Is the World?

◆

From the beginning of our life on Earth we are literally born into the world of nature. We are as we are born to be, according to our human nature. And from then onward, during the period of our formation or education, which is in fact lifelong, we may be said to remain in the world of nature.

For a period of nine months before we were born into the world we were being formed in our mother's womb. Even after our birth we remain in the metaphorical womb of family or school, in what is (or should be) a warm atmosphere of affection and friendship, until the time comes for us to enter the wider world, or what is called "human society."

We shed tears on emerging from the warmth of our mother's womb into the cold air outside and perhaps again on emerging from the warmth of family life into the cold air of an unfamiliar school. We have even more reason to shed tears—though by then we have been trained to repress them—on emerging from school, with all its ties of association and affection, into the adult world of men.

But what is this world of men in contrast to the world of nature, of family, and school? One somewhat pessimistic answer is that given by Newman in his autobiographical *Apologia pro Vita Sua*:

> I look out of myself into the world of men, and there I see a sight which fills me with unspeakable distress. The world seems simply to give the lie to that great truth of which my whole being is so full, and the effect upon me is, in consequence, as a matter of necessity, as confusing as if it denied that I am in existence myself. If I looked into a mirror and did not see my face, I should have

the sort of feeling which actually comes upon me
when I look into this living busy world and see
no reflection of its Creator.

He goes on to explain the reasons for his pessimism
at some length, but they belong to the Victorian world in
which he lived and died, a world to which we now look
back with optimistic nostalgia. It is enough for us to read
a daily newspaper to find reasons enough of our own for
pessimistic fears for the future, based on the tragic situation
of the world around us.

We see everywhere the triumph of the combined
powers of science and technology, politics and industry. We
see everywhere the rise of great cities—or rather what is now
termed the "megalopolis," the great metropolis or city-state
that consumes the surrounding countryside. "God made the
country," it was said, "but man made the town." But now, with
the advance of scientific materialism and practical atheism,
God is even being pushed out of the world of nature, while
men are engaged in constructing cities as palaces for the few

rich and prisons for the many poor or middle-class salaried (I almost said "slave") men and women.

Is it for such a world that we are formed in our mother's womb, and in the metaphorical wombs of family and school? Is it into such a world that we have to graduate from school? Yet haven't all those who constitute this world been through a formation similar to our own? How is it, then, that those formed in the ideal world of nature contribute to this real world of men that is so far removed from the ideals of both man and nature?

Further words of Newman in his *Apologia* are apposite. "What shall be said," he asks, "to this heart-piercing, reason-bewildering fact? I can only answer that either there is no Creator or this living society of men is in a true sense discarded from his presence." And so, he concluded, "the human race is implicated in some terrible aboriginal calamity. It is out of joint with the purposes of its Creator." Or, as Hamlet complains, "The time is out of joint. O cursed spite, that ever I was born to set it right!" For we are all in some way, to some extent, involved in the curse and are all called to share in the redemption of the world.

Such is the world students enter on their gradua-
tion from university, after undergoing the long process of
formation. Considering the greatness of the evil—and it is
even greater today than in Newman's time—what can we do
about it? Can we simply, like so many of our contemporaries,
abandon ourselves to the power of evil? Saint John pessimis-
tically observed, "The whole world is under the power of
the evil one." Are we to follow the Japanese proverb that
advises us to give way to a power greater than ourselves?

There are, it seems to me, at least two things that
we can do. One is simply to be aware of this evil and to
know something of its causes and development in the course
of human history. That should be one good effect of a
university education, especially a combined study of history
and literature. The other is to face the reality of the particular
employment in which we may find ourselves. The more we
come to know real human beings as individuals, rather than
in the mass, the more we will recognize that most of them are
basically good, like ourselves. We have no reason for setting

ourselves up in opposition to them as holier than thou.

In each situation we may find parallels to the warm atmosphere of home and school, those wombs of the spirit, especially when our work involves human relations on a small, family scale. We may even find ourselves working at a kindergarten or primary school so that we come into close contact with children. This is a most human and rewarding form of employment, even if the salary isn't so high as it would be for a less-personal position in a bank or insurance company. The more human and personal our work is, the better it is for us and our own personal growth, as well as for those we work with.

There is another task to which we should commit ourselves, whatever work we do. That is to bring as much nature, both physical and human nature, into our lives as possible. In particular, we should learn to prize plants and animals as well as our fellow human beings as precious gifts of God and thank and praise Him for them. It is not for us to combat the power of evil directly, as if we were little Saint Georges confronting the dragon. That power is too vast for us, and too unreal. But what we can do is nurture the natural good in ourselves and around us, by the grace of God.

ABOUT THE AUTHOR

Peter Milward was born in London in 1925, studied at Wimbledon College from 1933 to 1943, entered the Society of Jesus in 1943, studied philosophy at Heythrop College from 1947 to 1950, classical and English literature at Campion Hall, Oxford, from 1950 to 1954, and moved to Tokyo in 1954. He studied theology at St. Mary's College, Tokyo, from 1957 to 1961, was ordained priest in 1960, taught in the department of English literature at Sophia University from 1962 to 1996, then at Tokyo Junshin Women's College until 2002. At present he is professor emeritus at Sophia University and director of the Renaissance Institute, Tokyo.

Specializing in Shakespearian drama, he published

his first book, *An Introduction to Shakespeare's Plays*, in 1964, followed by *Christian Themes in English Literature* in 1967. As a result of further research at the Shakespeare Institute, Birmingham, from 1965 to 1966, he went on to publish *Shakespeare's Religious Background* in 1973, as well as *Biblical Themes in Shakespeare* (based on lectures given at Campion Hall, Oxford, in 1973). Then after research at the Huntington Library in California, as well as several other libraries, he brought out two companion volumes, *The Religious Controversies of the Elizabethan Age* in 1977 and *The Jacobean Age* in 1978. Then in 1987 he published *Biblical Influences in Shakespeare's Great Tragedies*, followed by three successive publications from St. Austin Press, *The Catholicism of Shakespeare's Plays* in 1997, *The Simplicity of the West* in 1998, and *Shakespeare's Apocalypse* in 2000.

He has also published books on Gerard Manley Hopkins, T. S. Eliot, Cardinal John Henry Newman, and G. K. Chesterton, in addition to many books or essays for Japanese students, numbering more than three hundred titles.